I get a lot of e-mail from *Dilbert* readers who ask questions like, "What's the story with the talking rat?" and "Where did that super-smart garbage man come from?" As a professional cartoonist, I am trained to recognize this situation as a natural market opportunity.

Well, saying I'm "trained" is probably an overstatement. When I was in eighth grade biology class, secretly doodling pictures of my teacher having an imagined romantic moment with the class skeleton, I didn't think of it as training per se. But it all worked out for the best . . . except for the skeleton, whose reputation never quite recovered.

Anyway, after eighth grade, a bunch of stuff happened to me (blah, blah, blah), and then I decided to create this book to feature many of the *Dilbert* regulars and semi-regulars. I'm leaving out some details about the whole sequence of events, but remember—a skeleton was involved—so you can come up with your own puns. You don't need me for the easy stuff.

S. Adams

ISBN: 0-8362-2879-0

THE DILBERT Bunch

A DILBERT® BOOK
BY
SCOTT ADAMS

Andrews McMeel Publishing

Kansas City

3/21/94 © United Feature Syndicate, Inc. (NYC)

4/28/94 © United Feature Syndicate, Inc. (NYC)

4/1/94 © United Feature Syndicate, Inc. (NYC)

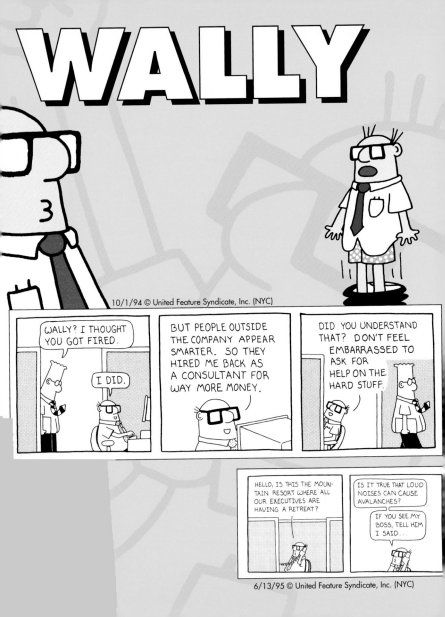

PHIL,
THE PRINCE OF INSUFFICIENT LIGHT

COME TO THE DARK SIDE, DILBERT. RENOUNCE ENGINEERING AND BECOME A MANAGER.

NEVER!!

YOUR TECHNICAL KNOWLEDGE IS GETTING STALE. YOU'RE BECOMING A GENERALIST... TAKE THE EASY PATH.

I BROUGHT YOU A SUITE OF APPLICATIONS THAT ALL WORK TOGETHER.

THAT'S UNNATURAL!!! BE GONE!!!

1/20/95 © United Feature Syndicate, Inc. (NYC)

IT'S "PHIL, THE PRINCE OF INSUFFICIENT LIGHT"!

I SAW YOU TAKE THAT CHAIR.

I SUMMON ALL THE DEMONS AND TROLLS OF HECK TO COME FORTH AND PUNISH YOU NOW!!!

12/9/93 © United Feature Syndicate, Inc. (NYC)

ELBONIANS

3/23/95 © United Feature Syndicate, Inc. (NYC)

3/28/95 © United Feature Syndicate, Inc. (NYC)